HIP-HOP AROUND THE WORLD

BEATS WITHOUT BORDERS

DR. MONICA B. MORALL-BAKER
CICELY LEWIS, EXECUTIVE EDITOR

Lerner Publications ◆ Minneapolis

LETTER FROM CICELY LEWIS

Dear Reader,

Hip-hop has been a part of my life from an early age. I remember using my brush as a microphone and rapping along with Salt-N-Pepa. Hip-hop influenced my fashion, way of speaking, and lifestyle. As a teacher, I shared Tupac's writings to teach poetry elements and Queen Latifah's "U.N.I.T.Y." to help my students better understand the works of poet Maya Angelou.

Cicely Lewis

As a librarian, I want to expose my students to literature that empowers them to take action and that amplifies voices of underrepresented groups. That is what hip-hop does. Hip-hop is more than beats and rhymes; it's a cultural force. For Black people, it's been a spotlight on social justice, and a canvas for our frustrations, joys, and creativity.

As you read the series, think about the power of hip-hop and how it all began. You've probably heard of Cardi B and Nicki Minaj, but who paved the way for them? Reflect on how this musical genre that began in the Black Community is now present around the world.

—Cicely Lewis, Executive Editor

Table of Contents

SPREADING HIP-HOP

Snoop Dogg carrying the torch at the 2024 Olympic Games

ON JULY 26, 2024, HIP-HOP SUPERSTAR SNOOP DOGG FACED ONE OF THE BIGGEST CROWDS OF HIS CAREER. Almost twenty-nine million viewers from around the world watched him at the Olympics. He carried the torch for the opening ceremony of the 2024 Olympic Games that were held in Paris, France.

Torchbearers are decided by an Olympic committee. They are usually people who have made an impact in their community or

Afrika Bambaataa (*right*) performing in London, England, in 1982

field. Snoop Dogg is a big name in hip-hop. He helped spread its sound in the early 1990s.

Hip-hop began in the 1970s in New York City. Soon after, its influence began to spread outside of the United States. In 1982 Afrika Bambaataa released the song "Planet Rock." It combined hip-hop with musical styles from all over the world. Within that same year, Bambaataa led the first international hip-hop tour to spread what he believed was hip-hop's message of peace and unity. Snoop Dogg and Bambaataa are just a couple of the artists who have not just made hip-hop popular but global.

CHAPTER 1

SAME MESSAGE, DIFFERENT BEAT

MC Lyte is an East Coast rapper. She helped lead the way for women in hip-hop.

HIP-HOP CULTURE QUICKLY GREW IN POPULARITY ALL OVER THE WORLD. Some countries developed their own hip-hop cultures by mixing American hip-hop with their own styles. In the United States, different regions added their own twist.

STATESIDE

Within the United States, there are multiple styles of hip-hop music. Hip-hop started on the East Coast in the Bronx, New York, in the 1970s. It was known for its hard-hitting rhythms and complex wordplay that focused on street life and social issues.

West Coast rap became popular in the 1980s. It was influenced by Black and Latinx communities in California. Its funk and electronic rhythms gave it an upbeat, party style. But its lyrics shed light on gang culture and social injustices such as police brutality.

Tupac is one of the best-known West Coast rappers in hip-hop history.

THE DIRTY SOUTH

The term "Dirty South" came from Atlanta rapper Cool Breeze in the early 1990s. He said the nickname refers to dirt roads in the South. He wanted to show that the Southern American states had just as much talent as the East and West Coasts.

Cool Breeze performing onstage at a 2016 music festival

The "Dirty South" style of rap hit the height of its popularity in the Southern United States in the mid-1990s. It was known for its fast beats, heavy bass tones, and colorful slang—language specific to a particular group or area.

ISLAND RHYTHMS

Latin American hip-hop draws on local musical influences such as samba, tango, and funk. These distinct drumbeats and rhythms have influenced many rappers and inspired new types of music such as reggaeton. Reggaeton combines Latin music with Jamaican sound and hip-hop. Artists such as Karol G, Bad Bunny, and Daddy Yankee have made this genre popular around the world.

Karol G is a Columbian singer, songwriter, and businessperson.

"Puerto Rico's relationship with music is everything. It's an island full of talent and if you grow up there, you grow up living and breathing music."

—Bad Bunny, 2018

MC Solaar is known for raps often set to a jazz backing track.

ACROSS THE SEA

Hip-hop is a major influence on music in countries in Europe. For example, France is considered hip-hop's second-largest market after the United States. Hip-hop started there as an imitation of American hip-hop, even down to copying American hip-hop fashion. But artists such as MC Solaar and the rap group IAM began to embrace French elements in their music. Some of these elements include an emphasis on poetry, storytelling, and fancy wordplay such as verlan (a form of French slang).

British hip-hop was influenced by both American and Caribbean music. Jamaican migrants introduced toasting, or talking over instrumental breaks in music, in the mid-1900s. Grime, or electronic dance music with fast breakbeats, became popular in Great Britain in the 2000s.

AFRICAN INFLUENCES

Since the 1990s Nigerian artists have copied American rappers such as Nas, Snoop Dogg, Tupac, and 50 Cent. Artists such as Dagrin and Reminisce blended the American sound with Afrobeats and Nigerian street music to create Yoruba rap. In the late 2010s Nigerian artists Burna Boy and Tems, and second-generation immigrant artists in the US such as Tobe Nwigwe, helped increase Afrobeats' popularity.

In the 1900s Ghanian artists such as Reggie Rockstone and Panji Anoff were influenced by American hip-hop. They created a

Burna Boy captivating the audience at the 2024 Glastonbury Festival

"I would find myself being inspired by things that [I] heard as a kid: Nigerian music or African music, some French music or some Jamaican music. When it's time for music to be made, it's almost like my ancestors just come into me and then it's them."

—Burna Boy, 2019

new style of music called hiplife. Ghanian hiplife music combines traditional African rhythms with rap and dance. Groups such as Talking Drums added their own lyrics and clothing styles to showcase their Ghanian identity. Artists such as Sarkodie keep Ghanaian music in the mainstream.

CHAPTER 2

GLOBAL POP CULTURE

Travis Scott helped popularize the slang word *lit* in hip-hop music.

HIP-HOP IS ONE OF THE TOP-SELLING GENRES OF MUSIC IN THE WORLD. It has influenced many other types of music as well. But hip-hop's reach extends far beyond music.

TALK THAT TALK

Hip-hop artists often create new words or change the meaning of existing words. Some of these words cross into mainstream culture. Commonly used words such as *dope, lit, bling,* and *fire* all have their roots in hip-hop.

ENTERTAINMENT

Hip-hop culture can be found in many forms of media. The 1990 sitcom *The Fresh Prince of Bel-Air* starred Will Smith, a Grammy-winning rapper. The show introduced hip-hop culture to a mainstream audience. Similarly, in 1995 the TV show *In*

In 2019 Will Smith recorded a hip-hop version of the song "Friend Like Me" from the Disney movie *Aladdin*.

REFLECT

Many slang words from hip-hop are used in mainstream culture. Why do you think certain hip-hop words are able to cross over into mainstream language?

the House came out, featuring rapper LL Cool J. Hip-hop saw a shift in audiences. It became more popular among people that weren't familiar with hip-hop. Fans can find many rap stars playing lead roles on TV shows and in movies.

In 2016 hip-hop hit the Broadway stage with Lin-Manuel Miranda's musical *Hamilton*. The production used rhymes, rhythms, and other elements of hip-hop culture to tell the life

Hamilton won the Tony for Best Musical in 2016.

"I mean, hip-hop's the language of revolution and it's our greatest American art form."

—Lin-Manuel Miranda, 2020

story of Alexander Hamilton, one of America's founders. As of 2024, *Hamilton* has won eleven Tony Awards, a top award in Broadway theater.

Many of Megan Thee Stallion's songs have gone on to become popular TikTok challenges.

DIGITAL MEDIA

Hip-hop is an important part of global digital culture. Artists use social media and digital platforms such as YouTube, TikTok, and Instagram to promote their music and connect with fans. Artists are judged as much on their streams and followers as they are on their sales. Viral media trends and dance challenges based on popular hip-hop songs are a way to promote hip-hop and extend its global reach.

SALES OR STREAMS?

The Recording Industry Association of America didn't originally count streams when giving out awards, but they changed their terms in 2013. As of 2024, fifteen hundred streams counted as one album or ten track sales.

REFLECT

Hip-hop culture has become a big part of mainstream culture. Where are some places you see hip-hop's influence?

The members of BTS light up Times Square on New Year's Eve in 2019.

FROM HIP-HOP TO K-POP

Beginning in the 2010s, Korean pop, commonly known as K-pop, brought hip-hop culture to a new generation of fans. South Korean boy bands such as BTS were inspired by Drake, Nas, the Notorious B.I.G., and Tupac. They incorporate hip-hop elements into their music.

CHAPTER 3

INTERNATIONAL ACTIVISM

Macklemore performing in 2024 in Melbourne, Australia

MUSIC IS OFTEN USED TO EXPRESS FEELINGS OF DISSATISFACTION ABOUT COMMUNITY AND SOCIETAL ISSUES. Hip-hop music is about sharing stories and giving power to those who may feel or often go unheard. Many hip-hop artists use their fame to bring attention to social issues and help others.

STATESIDE SUPPORTERS

In 2024 American rapper Macklemore partnered with an organization that helped Palestinians who had lost their homes because of war. He donated the profits from two of his songs to the organization. One of the songs featured Palestinian artists and the LA Palestinian Youth Choir.

In 2017 American rapper French Montana filmed a music video in Uganda. He saw the poor living conditions in the country and wanted to help. He donated money to a foundation in Uganda

French Montana appearing at the Teen Choice Awards in 2017

LIGHTING UP THE WORLD

Senegalese American rap star Akon started an organization called Akon Lighting Africa in 2014. The project raised money to provide basic needs such as electricity to families, hospitals, and schools. Through this project, he has helped provide solar energy to millions of people in Africa.

Aside from his work in hip-hop, Akon has lent his vocals to a wide range of genres, including songs by Whitney Houston and Lionel Richie.

that aimed to build a hospital to help pregnant women. He was later named a Global Citizen Ambassador for his donation. He said this is just the beginning of his mission to help women and children all over the world.

CHAMPIONING A CAUSE

In 2015 Puerto Rican rapper Residente was the first Latin American artist to be recognized by the Nobel Peace Summit. He has worked with Amnesty International to protect human rights all over the world. He has also worked with the United Nations Children's Fund to support children's education.

Residente wins the award for Best Short Form Music Video at the 2019 Latin Grammy Awards.

Maluma attending the 2017 Viña del Mar music festival

In 2017 Columbian rapper Maluma partnered with a charity in Chile. He wanted to help people who were affected by forest fires. He donated the proceeds from his performance at the Viña del Mar music festival to help forest fire victims.

REFLECT

In 2024 hip-hop celebrated its fiftieth anniversary. Why do you think hip-hop has continued to increase in popularity over the past five decades?

ADVOCATES FROM AFRICA

Ghanian artist Sarkodie created the Sarkodie Foundation in 2013. This organization offers programs for health, education, arts, and business to support underprivileged children in Ghana. Each year the group holds a festival to inspire young people to get involved with their communities.

Sarkodie is one of the leading hip-hop artists in Ghana.

In 2015 Kenyan rapper Octopizzo created the Octopizzo Foundation to help vulnerable young people in Kenya. This foundation helps young people develop their musical talent, showcases local craftworkers, and advocates to end violence against women and girls.

Octopizzo has worked with the United Nations to help refugee artists.

CHAPTER 4

THE FUTURE OF HIP-HOP

In 2024 Kendrick Lamar donated $200,000 to charities in Los Angeles, California.

HIP-HOP'S POPULARITY AROUND THE WORLD REACHES FAR BEYOND MUSIC. No one can predict the future of hip-hop. But certain things will help it remain a fan favorite.

THE VOICE OF THE VOICELESS

Hip-hop provides a voice for social change. In 2024 Mozambique artist Iveth wrote a song to honor the seventy-fifth anniversary of the Universal Declaration of Human Rights. This song traces the history of human rights all over the world. It also inspires people to think about the future of civil rights.

Black and Japanese American artist Aisha Fukushima calls herself a raptivist, or rap activist. She created the RAPtivism project to shed light on the connection between hip-hop, female empowerment, and activism. She has partnered with organizations such as the American Civil Liberties Union and Humanity in Action to advocate for human rights.

HIP-HOP'S LASTING LEGACY

Many countries honor the legacy of hip-hop. In 2021 the United States Congress made November National Hip-Hop

REFLECT

Hip-hop has always provided a voice for underrepresented people. Why do you think hip-hop's message resonates with people from all over the world?

History Month. In 2023 the National Museum of Ghana opened the exhibit *Culture Curators: Hip-Hop 50.* This exhibit honors hip-hop's fiftieth anniversary.

Hip-hop has changed communities, empowered historically marginalized groups, and provided a platform to unite artists and fans all over the world. Hip-hop will continue to influence local and global cultures for generations to come.

The city of Atlanta, Georgia, celebrates hip-hop's fiftieth anniversary in 2023 with performances by artists such as T.I. and Omeretta the Great (*above*).

Glossary

advocate: to publicly support a specific cause or be a figure that supports a cause

Afrobeats: a style of popular music that uses elements of African music and jazz, soul, and funk

injustice: lack of fairness or justice

mainstream: something that is regarded as normal or is the dominant trend in opinion or media

marginalized: an unrepresented person or a person that is treated as unimportant

platform: an opportunity or position of influence to communicate ideas or opinions

police brutality: the use of unwarranted or excessive force by police

second-generation immigrant: a person who has at least one foreign-born parent

stream: music or something else played directly from the internet

verlan: a type of French slang that flips syllables

viral: quickly and widely spread or popularized especially through social media

vulnerable: at-risk or in need of special care, support, or protection

Source Notes

9 Iman Amrani, "'We Grow Up Breathing Music': How Puerto Rico Became a Pop Superpower," *Guardian* (US edition), July 12, 2018, https://www.theguardian.com/music/2018/jul/12/grow-up-breathing-music-puerto-rico-pop-superpower-despacito.

12 Joey Akan, "With *African Giant*, Burna Boy's Crossover Is Complete," *Fader*, July 29, 2019, https://www.thefader.com/2019/07/29/burna-boy-african-giant-essay-review.

16 Heran Mamo, "Lin-Manuel Miranda Explains How 'Hamilton' Serves as a 'Love Letter to Hip-Hop' That He Grew Up On," *Billboard*, July 7, 2020, https://www.billboard.com/music/rb-hip-hop/lin-manuel-miranda-apple-music-interview-9414834/.

Reading List

AP News: Living in a Hip-Hop World
https://projects.apnews.com/features/2023/hip-hop-50th-history/living-in-a-hip-hop-world.html

Britannica Kids: World Music
https://kids.britannica.com/kids/article/world-music/399997

Elizabeth, Jordannah. *A Child's Introduction to Hip-Hop: The Beats, Rhymes, and Roots of a Musical Revolution*. New York: Black Dog & Leventhal, 2023.

Holleran, Leslie. *BTS: K-Pop's Biggest Headliners*. Minneapolis: Lerner Publications, 2025.

Kid Museum: Reggaeton Music
https://kid-museum.org/maker-playground/culture-spotlight-reggaeton-music/

Library of Congress Blogs: Celebrating Fifty Years of Hip-Hop with Children's Literature and Activities
https://blogs.loc.gov/families/2023/11/celebrating-fifty-years-of-hip-hop-with-childrens-literature-and-activities/

Scaletta, Kurtis. *Lin-Manuel Miranda: Raising Theater to New Heights*. New York: Random House, 2021.

Williams, Jarrett. *Hip-Hop: The Beat of America*. New York: First Second, 2024.

Index

Photo Acknowledgments

Image credits: AP Photo/Marcus Brandt, p. 4; David Corio/Getty Images, p. 5; Everett Collection Inc/Alamy, p. 6; Pat Johnson/MediaPunch Inc/Alamy, p. 7; Paras Griffin/Getty Images, p. 8; AP Photo/Chris Tuite/imageSPACE/MediaPunch, p. 9; AP Photo/ANTHONY BEHAR/SIPA USA, p. 10; AP Photo/Scott A Garfitt, p. 11; AP Photo/Amy Harris, p. 13; Frazer Harrison/Getty Images, p. 14; AP Photo/Evan Agostini, p. 15; AP Photo/Amy Harris/Invision, p. 16; AP Photo/Ben Hider/Invision, p. 18; Morgan Hancock/Getty Images, p. 19; AP Photo/Phil McCarten/Invision, p. 20; AP Photo/Henri Collot/SIPA, p. 21; AP Photo/Richard Brian/Sipa USA, p. 22; Marcelo Benitez/Latincontent/Getty Images, p. 23; Ollie Millington/WireImage/Getty Images, p. 24 (top); Richard Blanshard/Getty Images, p. 24 (bottom); AP Photo/Ricardo Rubio/Europa Press, p. 25; Paras Griffin/Getty Images, p. 27. Design elements: spxChrome/Getty Images; Goji/Shutterstock; BormanT/Shutterstock; Yurals Art/Shutterstock; topform/Shutterstock; Sergio Gasp/Shutterstock; redgreystock/Shutterstock; Vanzyst/Shutterstock.

Cover: Ollie Millington/Getty Images; Taylor Hill/Getty Images.

For Mom and Dad, and to Dwight, my love

Lerner Publications Company
An imprint of Lerner Publishing Group, Inc.
241 First Avenue North
Minneapolis, MN 55401 USA

For reading levels and more information, look up this title at www.lernerbooks.com.

Main body text set in Aptifer Sans LT Pro.
Typeface provided by Linotype AG.

Editor: Annie Zheng **Photo Editor:** Elena Mai
Lerner team: Martha Kranes

Library of Congress Cataloging-in-Publication Data

Names: Morall-Baker, Monica B., author.
Title: Hip-hop around the world : beats without borders / Dr. Monica B. Morall-Baker.
Description: Minneapolis : Lerner Publications, 2026. | Series: Hip-hop culture | Includes bibliographical references and index. | Audience: Ages 9–14 | Audience: Grades 4–6 | Summary: "Since hip-hop began, it has spread to countries around the world and grown digitally. From viral videos and streams to its influence in Europe, Africa, and more, discover more about hip-hop around the world"— Provided by publisher.
Identifiers: LCCN 2024045895 (print) | LCCN 2024045896 (ebook) | ISBN 9798765659885 (library binding) | ISBN 9798765684245 (paperback) | ISBN 9798765678176 (epub)
Subjects: LCSH: Rap (Music)—History and criticism—Juvenile literature. | Hip-hop—Juvenile literature.
Classification: LCC ML3531 .M6614 2025 (print) | LCC ML3531 (ebook) | DDC 782.421649—dc23/eng/20241001

LC record available at https://lccn.loc.gov/2024045895
LC ebook record available at https://lccn.loc.gov/2024045896

Manufactured in the United States of America
1-1011689-53635-3/6/2025